AN ALPHINGTON A

Pauline Aplin and Jeanne Gaskell

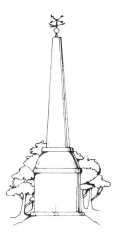

OBELISK PUBLICATIONS

PLATE ACKNOWLEDGEMENTS

Rev M. Bate for page 11, Mr P. Branson for page 62, Mr P. Collins for page 6, Mrs D. Lake for pages 15, 37 and 38, Mr Bert Moxey for pages 10, 12, 45, 58, 59 and 61, Mr H. Seward for pages 4, 7, 9, 13, 14, 17, 24-29, 36 and 53, Mrs J. Stockman for pages 34 and 51, Mrs H. Webb for page 42, Chips Barber for pages 18 and 64, Express & Echo for pages 55, 58, 59 and 63, Pauline Aplin for all other pictures.

This book is dedicated to the memory of our grandparents, Charles and Alice Coles, the Coles family having lived in Alphington for many generations dating back to the 1500s.

Other Obelisk Publications

Around & About the Haldon Hills, Chips Barber
The Lost City of Exeter, Chips Barber
Diary of a Dartmoor Walker, Chips Barber
Adventure Through Red Devon, Raymond B Cattell
An Exeter Boyhood, Frank Retter
The Torbay Book, Chips Barber
Under Sail through South Devon & Dartmoor, R. B. Cattell
The Great Walks of Dartmoor, Terry Bound
Ide, Bill Rowland
Diary of a Devonshire Walker, Chips Barber
Rambling in the Plymouth Countryside, Lister & Woolley
The Great Little Dartmoor Book, Chips Barber
Tales of the Unexplained in Devon, Judy Chard
The Great Little Exeter Book, Chips Barber
The DevonAir Book of Family Walks, Chips Barber
Running in Devon, John Legge

Memories of Newton Abbot, Elsie Townsend
Albert Labbett's Crediton Collection
DevonAir Book of Haunted Happenings, Judy Chard
Made in Devon, Chips Barber & David FitzGerald
Dartmoor in Colour, Chips Barber
Burgh Island & Bigbury Bay, Chips Barber & Judy Chard
Dark and Dastardly Dartmoor, Sally and Chips Barber
Talking about Topsham, Sara Vernon
Peter Tully's Pictures of Paignton

First Published in 1988 by Obelisk Publications,
2 Church Hill, Pinhoe, Exeter, Devon
Printed in Great Britain by Penwell Ltd, Parkwood, Callington, Cornwall.
©Pauline Aplin and Jeanne Gaskell 1988

Alphington Village Devon

This picture of the Church must have been taken before the First World War because it does not show the War Memorial. On the left is Tozers Cottage, now a Chemist shop, next to that is Pixie Cottage (not shown) and then, turning left is Clapperbrook Lane which ran to the west bank of the canal at Salmon Pool Bridge in Alphington Parish. It is thought that the lane was part of an ancient route by which travellers coming from London could bypass the walled city of Exeter on their way to Plymouth via what is now Barrack Road and Salmon Pool Lane, crossing the river at a nearby ford called Madford. Before the Canal was built a track led directly to Clapperbrook Lane, probably then with its Clapper Bridge and brook ford alongside as at Postbridge. The lane was at one time known as Watry Lane.

Alphington War Memorial and Church.

The War Memorial Cross was erected in proud memory of the 30 men of the Parish of Alphington who gave their lives in the Great War. This was out of a total population of about 1,150.

There is no mention of an Alphington church in Domesday Book (1086) but it is known there was a church soon after 1100 because Charles Worthy in "Suburbs of Exeter" states that from a document dated soon after, and preserved by the College of Arms, the revenues of St Michael, Alphington, were appropriated to Plympton Priory by William Avenal, Lord of the Manor of Okehampton, and probably looked after by a chaplain from Exeter Cathedral. This is the first mention of the dedication of the church to St Michael, which is one of great antiquity and can be traced back twelve centuries.

In 1877 a report on preliminary inspection induced the church wardens and the Rev Dr Dennett to appoint an architect and to call a parish meeting at which the Lord of the Manor, the Earl of Devon, took the chair. The architect's report revealed that few of the walls remained at right angles to each other and that the south wall was out of perpendicular, having been forced outwards by the pressure of the roof, which itself was in a most dilapidated condition and the roof timbers decayed. The chancel was in advanced disrepair. The internal vaults and the ground outside from excessive burials had rendered the church unwholesome, so much so that whilst engaged in the survey, the smell was at one time so bad as to produce nausea. The architect, therefore, recommended that no new burials be allowed in the old churchyard and that the vaults inside the church be cemented over, also that proper provision be made for heating the church. The old pulpit was "simply a wooden deformity" and the furniture and hassocks were in a dreadful condition. The interior aspect of the church was spoilt by pews up to five feet high, seen in two photos in the church.

By contrast the twelfth century Beer stone font is one of the finest of its period in Devon. Enriched with scrollwork and arcading, it has a quaint procession round the top showing St Michael or some other dragon hunter, an archer, a huntsman with two quarrelsome dogs, a grotesque carrying a hare on a pole, a dragon snarling at a bird, and lastly the dragon himself with an arrow through his throat. So much admired is this font that London copied it for Temple Church.

The church was reopened on 25 July 1878 with a dedication service attended by the Bishop of Exeter. Messrs Stephens & Son of Exeter did the work at an eventual cost of £4,400. The incumbent Rev Butterfield died at the end of 1879 and when the Rev E. J. G. Dupuis took over early in 1880 he found himself the rector of a beautiful church in a fine old parish!

Bishop Westall, as Archdeacon of Exeter, visited Alphington Church on the Sunday before Advent 1957 and wrote, "I am impressed by the loving care which has been bestowed upon this church. Everything is most carefully tended yet there is nothing of the museum here. The happy life of the Family of God in this place says much for those who have ministered and minister here."

A disaster occurred in Alphington on Monday, 6 October 1986 in the early hours of the morning when, by an act of arson, a terrible fire raged, severely damaging the roof, centre and south aisles, vestry and organ and it was estimated that the cost of repairs would be in the region of £250,000. The tower, which was repaired three years before at a cost of £18,000 was not affected by the blaze. The fire started in the organ area in the vestry, and almost half the slates on the main roof had to be removed to get to the seat of the fire. Many people worked all day to clean the black tar from a section of the seating and on 7 October the bells pealed and, with emergency lighting and a piano installed, the Rector, Rev Mark Bate, held a special service attended by about 150 people. Following the restoration, the first service in the church was on the eve of the feast of St Michael on Monday 28 September 1987.

This picture shows the view from the top of the Church Tower and looks along Ide Lane. The Institute can be seen on the right and at the end of the lane Sobeys Farm—the last owner was Percy Dadd who used his horses to drive the judges to the Guildhall for the Assizes. The farm was sold for housing development and the field opposite used for the new school. In the distance on the right can be seen the Teign Valley Railway crossing the far end of Ide Lane.

ALPHINGTON.

This view is also from the top of the Church Tower looking down the main road through the village. On the right can be seen both Pixie Cottage and Tozers Cottage, and after the trees Rosemont with the flats. Opposite, behind the row of cottages is Buscoves now Brookfield Gardens. In the centre towards the back are open fields which are now the St Thomas High School and to the right the fields have now been swallowed up by the Marsh Barton Trading Estate.

Looking south and southwest, again from the Church Tower, this picture shows the Rectory Garden in the foreground and, on the right, Bartletts and Aldens Farm. The road to Shillingford can be clearly seen in the top right hand corner.

Alphington May 5. 1939.

Every year a great deal of money was spent on the Church Bells on oil and leather, ropes and repairs. Individual bells were recast or had new parts. In 1725 a treble bell was added. In 1749 the existing five bells were recast and a peal of eight bells was hung, cast by Bilbie of Cullompton at a cost of £108.12s.8d. It was then the largest peal in Devon, and the first peal cast together in the county. In 1939 the bells which had hung on wooden frames were re-hung on metal frames. The picture shows the bells prior to re-hanging with, from left to right, Messrs J. J. Brewer, Dymond, F. Brewer, Lake, Rogers, Grimes, Cornelius, H. Brewer, Moxey, Pike, Osborne, Perkins, Coles and Rogers.

Alphington Bells. 1749-1939.

There were three regular ringing days for which the ringers were paid: 5 November; 29 May (Oak-apple Day, Birthday and return of Charles II who landed at Dover on 26 May 1660); and the King's birthday. There were also special occasions such as in 1685 when Monmouth was taken, 1687, 1690 and 1693 'when the Lord Bishop passed by', in 1704 and 1808 (Blenheim and Oudenarde) for 'The good news from Malborro'; in 1707 for the Union of England and Scotland; in 1761 'for taking ye Havannah'. The picture shows the bells prior to re-hanging and the Rector Preb B. C. Bennett and two of the workmen.

This is the outing in 1911 of the Alphington Society of Ringers. Some of the men in the picture are: Messrs Westcott, Rogers, Brewer, Pillar, Osborne, Dymond, Coles and Pike.

This picture of Church Road shows Ye Olde Alphington Bakery and Cafe and the Paper Shop. The Hatswell family ran the bakery and later the Pollards when, as children, we went between the two shops (where the dog's head is seen protruding) and down the alleyway which led directly into the bakery. Here we could buy buns for a farthing and a ha'penny and the smell of the bread was gorgeous.

THE RECTORY ALPHINGTON. 23497

In our young days the Rectory was the centre of village life, we danced the Maypole, we held our Fetes there, we collected our Coronation and Jubilee Mugs from there and it was the focal point of our activities. Things changed in the war, however, when the field below the Rectory and the field on the other side of the road, where the Raglans estate has since been built, was taken over by the troops. Nissan huts were erected in both fields and during the war this was home to the ATS who worked in the Pay Office at the By Pass Camp at Middlemoor. After the war the huts were taken over by homeless families until they were re-housed in the early 1950s.

The first clock was installed in 1710 at a cost of £16.1s.5d. The clockmaker was paid 15 shillings a year to wind and maintain the clock. In 1716 the Sexton took over the winding. A new clock was installed in 1798 at a cost of £12.12s.0d. and 10/6d was paid for maintenance. Before the war the Sibley family erected the illuminated cross shown on the church tower and this could be seen for miles around. The cross was removed, probably during the war because it was such a good landmark.

ALPHINGTON.CROSS. 5340

There are three thirteenth century wayside crosses in Alphington Parish. The best known, Alphington Cross, stood at the corner north-east of the junction of Alphington Road and Cowick Lane, but between the world wars was moved to a grass triangle on the south-west side. It has been moved 'again, owing to road reconstruction, and now stands on a green on the east side of Alphington Road. This cross gave the name to Cross or Crosse House, Cross Cottage and Cross View—from which, however, the cross could never have been seen!

Dr R. K. Fortescue Foulkes who, before the last war, lived at Belvil or Belleville, No 1 Church Road (now re-named 'Fairfax'), said that the head of the war memorial cross was found at the corner of Mill Lane, and fitted to a modern shaft. Subsequently, the shaft of an old cross, together with a millstone, was dug up in the garden of Belvil; this shaft now leans against the north-west buttress of the church tower. The millstone was incorporated into a sunken rock garden made by Dr Foulkes.

The third cross is Little John's Cross on the Dunsford Road which, presumably, gave the name to Crossmead, just outside the parish boundary.

EXETER ROAD AND OLD CROSS, ALPHINGTON.

The villagers had, at one time, to walk this road to Marsh Barton to catch the green City of Exeter buses to town, the alternative being the red Devon General buses. The orchards on the left of the picture are before the building of St Thomas School and on the right, the near derelict cottage was once used as home by Lofty and Ginger, well known 'Gentlemen of the Road'. All the cottages were removed and replaced by Government Buildings which houses the Ministry of Agriculture and Fisheries etc.

GIDLEYS—*This is thought to be the oldest house in Alphington and is built of cob and thatch. The house was named after Bartholomew Gidley who settled in Alphington sometime before 1612 and the family disappears from the Alphington records in 1695. It was, up to 1920, a perfect example of an early English farmhouse. It is thought that the panelling in the dining-room came from the old box pews which were removed from the church in 1876. Gidleys previously had its own home farm round about it, but this was thrown into Sobeys when Mr John Coles became the tenant in the middle 1850s.*

In the garden of Gidleys is the ruin of a stone outbuilding some four feet long which was used for storing thatching materials. The Cottage is in the form of a capital 'T', and in the base of the upright is a large barn used partly as a garage, but largely taken over as home for barn owls. The original pump is still in situ, and was in constant use up to the 1960s and could still be used if needed. Even under extreme conditions the well has never been known to run dry.

This postcard is dated 1930 before Webb's Garage and the houses opposite, where Harry Webb eventually lived, were built. The field in which the houses were built was, during the middle of the nineteenth century, let for strip grazing. There were many such fields used in this way in Alphington. The card is actually signed by Jocelyn Foulkes who marked her home with an 'X' on the far right next to the railway bridge. Mandrake Farm and shippen is seen first left. John Wandrake appears as a Devon estate tenant in the early 1700s and later the property is listed as Wandrakes, and later still the W seems to have been inverted and became Mandrake. Many of the properties in the village took their names from the families who originally owned them.

Railway Bridge, Alphington Cross.

The Teign Valley line was opened on 1 July 1903 when a one-track line ran from St David's Station through St Thomas to Alphington Halt and then on through Ide, Longdown and Dunsford to Christow. There were 24 bridges and two tunnels, the most important of which was Perridge, 829 yards long, the other being Culver 250 yards long. Later the line was continued to Ashton, Trusham, Chudleigh, Chudleigh Knighton, Heathfield and so to Newton Abbot. It is a great pity that this picturesque line was axed; we quite regularly used it to get to Torquay and Goodrington, changing trains at Newton Abbot. We also used the line in the evenings when we caught the train to St Thomas Station where we changed trains for Dawlish Warren. After an hour in the sea we came back the same way, how convenient! The railway line and bridge have since been removed.

Mile End Cottage and Village, Alphington.

This is Devonia Terrace, now re-named Church Road, where the iron railings and gates were removed from the houses during the war and used for munitions. First right is Mile End Cottage, and second right is Willow Cottage where Charlie Edwards, our shoe repairer, lived with his family. Opposite is the petrol station and the white building was Rose Cottages, two very old cottages which were unfortunately demolished and are now part of Rawle Gammon and Baker.

Mile End Cottage
Exeter
Once the Home of Dickens

Mile End Cottage's claim to fame is that the great Charles Dickens once rented it for his parents and a plaque on the house verifies the fact. It is obvious from a letter that Charles Dickens wrote to Mr Mitton, in March 1839, that he was pleased with his find.

"I do assure you that I am charmed with the place and the beauty of the country round about, though I have not seen it under very favourable circumstances, for it snowed when I was there this morning and blew bitterly from the east yesterday. I shall be quite sorry to leave it . . . the house is on the high road to Plymouth and, though in the very heart of Devonshire, there is as much long-stage and posting life as you would find in Piccadilly. The situation is charming—meadows in front, an orchard running parallel to the garden hedge, richly-wooded hills closing in the prospect behind, and away to the left, before a splendid view of the hill on which Exeter is situated, the Cathedral towers rising up to the sky in the most picturesque manner possible."

To his biographer, John Forster, he wrote:
"I almost forget the number of rooms; but there is an excellent parlour with two other rooms on the ground floor. There is really a beautiful little room over the parlour which I am furnishing as a drawing room and there is a splendid garden. The paint and wallpaper throughout is new and fresh and cheerful-looking. The place is clean beyond all description and the neighbourhood, I suppose, the most beautiful in this most beautiful of English counties."

Although they were pleased with the cottage at first, within a few weeks Mrs Dickens started to complain. The rent was £20 a year, the furniture cost £70 and the coal cost £6.6s a ton. The landlady's name was Mary Pannell; her husband Nathaniel died in 1823 and she died in 1845; their vault is near the tower door and old stoke-hole of the church. The Dickens household consisted of John Dickens, his wife Elizabeth, their youngest son Augustus, the servant Hester Drinkwater, and their dog, Dash. John Dickens had been a clerk in the Navy Pay Office. He was a most improvident man and his life was spent in the midst of financial difficulties. He was committed to Marshalsea debtor's prison but, after quite a time there, was released in 1824, after paying his debts from a legacy from his mother. Charles was then 12 and suffered acutely from his father's imprisonment. John Dickens was no sooner free of one debt that he incurred another. (Mr Micawber in "David Copperfield" is said to be based on him.) In 1839 Charles felt obliged to send his parents away from London and rented Mile End Cottage for them.

John Dickens made some friends in Alphington, including Samuel Dyer Knott, who lived at Bartlett's, John Hele the postmaster and John Coles, our great grandfather. He was described as a chatty and pleasant companion, possessed of a varied fund of anecdotes and a genuine vein of humour.

Mile End Cottage, Alphington, Exeter.
(House in which Charles Dickens
lived with his parents.)

The petrol station on the right hand side in Devonia Terrace has now become Queen Street Carpets. Where the Ronuk floor polish advert is located is Cross View. In about 1790 there was a rope walk here, the ropes being supplied to shipping at the Port of Exeter and made by an Alphington rope maker.

On 22 October 1960 the Alphin Brook, normally quiet, gentle and picturesque, turned into a ferocious river and many people, including old age pensioners, had to be rescued by boat. Some people were taken in by neighbours and others went to stay with relatives, and those who had escaped damage were quick to offer a helping hand. People whose houses sustained damage were given chits entitling them to free coal to help dry out their homes and this was paid for by the church. A Harvest Supper had been arranged for the Saturday but this was cancelled and the food delivered to some of the people who had been affected by the flooding.

BY THE STREAM, ALPHINGTON.

Copyright.
ALPH. 2

This leafy lane leads to the fields beside the Alphin Brook (now Alphin Brook Road) and in younger days we spent a lot of time in the fields, picnicing and fishing. In those days, when the brook was high, many trout were seen in the water, and sometimes even a salmon! The Brook, as it was always known, rises in Holcombe Burnell, and a tributary flows down from Whitestone east through Ide and Alphington to the Exe. The tributary from Whitestone crosses the original Okehampton road at Nadderwater, about two miles north of Ide, and is known as Nadder Brook. The two streams meet near Pocombe Bridge on the Moretonhampstead road and then flow past Ide, where the Fordland Brook adds its flow. The Alphin Brook itself

THE BROOK. ALPHINGTON. 2350.

flows down the west side of the canal tow path south of Countess Weir Bridge and then disappears into a pyll or creek called Matford Brook, which joins the Exe below Countess Weir. Probably before the canal was made the brook flowed into the Exe about half way between St James Weir, or Salmon Pool, and Countess Weir. Oliver says (about 1824)—The Alphington Brook had been carried through on an aqueduct of iron cylinders laid three feet below the canal into the bed of the river. This picture shows the view from Mill Lane Bridge towards the Church.

In 1699 a tree growing near the main bridge over the Alphin Brook was sold by the authorities for five shillings to repair the then wooden bridge. About 30 years later a stone bridge was built with twin arches which may well have impeded the flow as floods destroyed many houses. The bridge was replaced by a single arched bridge in 1843, built to the specification of James Green, the chief surveyor of county bridges, and engineer of the Canal Basin in 1830. The work on the bridge was carried out by Richard & Clement Chapple of Kennford at a cost of £250. The pictures show the widening of the bridge in 1926.

Brooklands Hotel was previously Brooklands Farm. In the 1930s the hotel was seriously damaged by fire when the thatch caught alight. It is now the site of the premises of Rawle, Gammon and Baker. The next property down the road was Rose Cottages, and the end house with hoarding is the start of Devonia Terrace, since changed to Church Road.

Alphington Village

J.W.S. 1636

This peaceful scene shows Scanes Old Bakery with a balcony and a row of nine cottages known as Scanes Cottages which were below what was a Blacksmiths and Wheelwrights Shop, Perkins and Sons. It is now owned by Colletts. Opposite can be seen the Rectory Wall where, during the Crimean War, men met on a Sunday afternoon to hear the latest news from the front as newspapers were scarce and costly.

CHUDLEIGH ROAD, ALPHINGTON.

On the right in the picture, Alden's Farm in Chudleigh Road was named after the Rev Alden, a former rector who owned the farm. It is said that at one time there was a tunnel leading directly from the farm to the church—very convenient on a wet day! Opposite is a thatched house named Belvoir.

FIRE AT ALPHIGNTON FEBUARY 13 1909

A serious fire happened on 13 February 1909 when Scanes Bakery and cottages were burnt down leaving 40 people homeless. Apparently the fire engines took a long time to arrive because all the firemen were at a football match! It was left to a local builder to go off on his bicycle to the fire alarm in Alphington Road. In the meantime some of the men went into the church and rang all the bells and so called the firemen back from Raglands field where they were playing football. Despite all efforts the cottages were destroyed and later replaced by a row of more modern houses.

FIRE AT ALPHIGNTON FEBUARY 13 1909 G

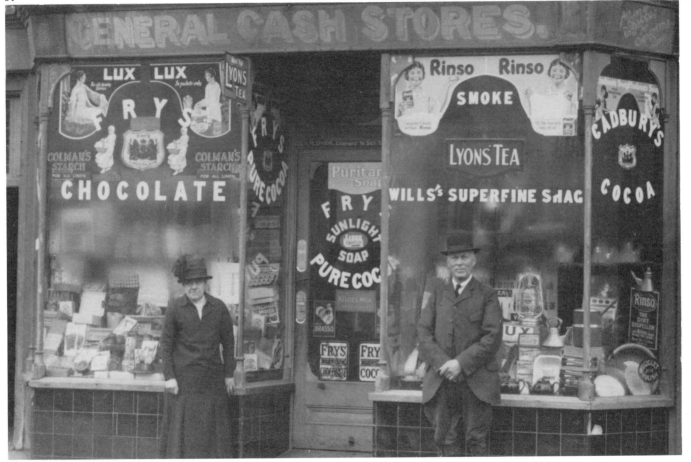

Mr and Mrs Grayer are seen standing outside their General Store in the early 1930s. The shop, now a bakery, stands in Chudleigh Road opposite the lychgate.

View of Alphington, beyond Church.

On the left of the picture is Scanes Cottages in Chudleigh Road. The entrance to the churchyard, right, now has a lychgate erected by Miss Mitchell in memory of her family.

CHUDLEIGH RD ALPHINGTON 23501.

This is another shop in Chudleigh Road and, on the corner of Ide Lane on the left, is Parr's Cottages, the New Inn and the headmaster's house. The shadow of the churchyard hedge is on the right.

A slight accident at the Schoolmaster's house beside the school! This was once the site of the Church House also the Red Lion and the Vernon's Head (later changed to the Admiral Vernon). On 15 September 1871 a great fire destroyed the Admiral Vernon, two adjoining houses occupied by Messrs Nosworthy & Buckbet, and a butcher's shop belonging to Mr Fry. The landlord's family fortunately escaped. Four fire engines attended, the West of England (2), Norwich and Sim but scarcity of water prevented them from being brought into play for some time, then only two could be used the others acting as feeders, supplying water from the brook. The fire burnt itself out and only the bare walls remained. A court used to be held at the Admiral Vernon in the seventeenth century which lawyers differentiated into a Court Leet for Criminal cases and a Court Baron to regulate parish affairs.

Alphington School and Village.

This is an early view of the old school which was replaced in 1987 by a new school in Ide Lane. The older part of the school was the site of the Church House, first mentioned in 1499, which appears to have stood on a corner, presumably Ide Lane, and to have been thatched. It was apparently 'a noble Tudor-fronted building' and used for manorial and parochial meetings and by the Admiral Vernon Inn. It was burnt down in 1875 and the land was afterwards sold for the site of this school. The first parochial school was established in 1812 for the education of the poor of this and adjoining parishes and was supported by voluntary subscription. When the Board School was opened in 1878 the old school became the reading room and then the Church Institute.

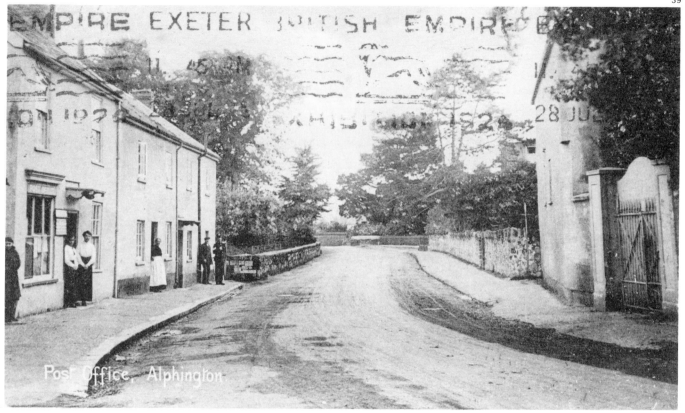

Post Office, Alphington

The first Post Office was at the corner of Ide Lane, and later moved northwards. William Searle, a market gardener, took over the site but by about 1872 the New Inn had replaced this. Charles Coles, a well known bellringer and sexton for nearly 50 years, married Searle's daughter, Sarah, and took over the New Inn in 1890. The Post Office moved further down Church Road as shown in the picture, now a paper shop, and from there to Cross View. Recently it has moved again to Church Road, near the Cross View corner. Near right is Rosemont, the home of the Heale family for many years, now turned into flats as is the garden behind the wall and named after the house. It could easily be Mr Pike himself standing talking to the police Sgt outside his cottage. This is long before he built his new house Buscoves next door and extended his market garden onto what is now Brookfield Gardens.

The state of the road surface is very poor in this view of Ide Lane looking towards the Church. The house near right is called Ventlake and at the end on the left is Parr's Cottages which were demolished and replaced by Lockfield Court flats next to the New Inn.

This is Midway Terrace, a row of workmen's cottages approached from Ide Lane, ending near the Teign Valley railway line. There was an incendiary bomb dropped here during the war and the only casualty was a Mr Rossiter who lived in one of the cottages. He threw out the incendiary which had gone through the roof of his home, and the local ARP came and took him to the R D & E Hospital.

Harry Webb's Garage opened in 1931. Beyond it can be seen the Walnut tree at Mandrake Farm which received a great deal of attention from young and old alike at a certain time of year!

Double Locks, Exeter.

It is interesting to note how Italian 'know-how' was used to advantage in a part of Alphington. Traffic up and down canals was made possible when locks were developed on the continent in the Middle Ages. These 'pound-locks' were at first rather clumsily fitted with a single opening gate at either end. Leonardo de Vinci improved them by inventing the familiar double gates which close to a mitred fit, and are swung open or shut with long balance beams. Leonardo's pound-lock was first used in Britain on the Exeter Ship Canal in 1563-6. Another interesting fact is that the mast of HMS Exeter, which took part in the battle of the River Plate in the Second World War, forms the two arms of the gates at Double Locks Hotel which is, of course, in Alphington Parish.

The house in Chudleigh Road, now known as The Gables, was originally Exon View and one of the old Alphington Manor houses. Dating from about 1730, and added to in 1820, it now has 22 rooms. The house was at one time used as a prison for those awaiting hanging from an old Oak Tree at the four cross way on the Shillingford Road. There is still in existence the unique tunnel of some 20-30 yards, from the one time wine cellar through which those to be executed were taken. Thereafter the bodies were brought back along Hangman's Lane (now known as Markhams Lane) and buried on the opposite side of the road to the house. The cellar is now a bedroom and the old wooden door, still propped up against the wall of the tunnel, has been replaced by a thick glass door. At the Markhams Lane end is an iron gate. The house was once owned and occupied by the Wippel-Hex, a well known local family.

This is the Alphington bellringers' entry in the Exeter Water Carnival which it is thought to have been a single event. As can be seen it is a very ambitious portrayal of Alphington Church Tower— worthy of first prize we think! Most of the faces are obscured but Alex Rogers is clearly visible in the centre.

During the 1930s Alphington had its own Carnival and also entered floats in the St Thomas' Carnival. This photo was taken in Cross View and shows Alphington Children's Carnival around 1935 taken outside the General Store which was run by Vera Cann and later by Mr Ashleigh.

"Alphington".

This peaceful scene in Chudleigh Road shows the Admiral Vernon Inn, near right and Bartletts, first left. The sign post pointing right in the far distance shows the way to Shillingford, passing the site of the Cattle and Horse Fairs (the largest in Devon) which were held here during the first half of the nineteenth century. During these times there were twelve public or 'bush' houses open in the village for the sale of beer and cider, and the Admiral Vernon Inn cooked as many as 60 geese during the two days of the fair, as well as other joints. The fair was in the road from the bridge leading to Shillingford near Clapperbrook Lane. But this was an unsatisfactory site and the fair was removed to a field near at hand, until it ceased to be held in 1870. Fairfield Road commemorates the site of the fairs.

The W.I. had a thriving Drama Team and in March 1936 they won the Shield for the first time with a mark of 98 percent having lost one mark for 'poor play' and one mark for the make-up on the maid's face! The play was produced by Mrs Ellen Coles. Pictured from left are Mrs Coles, Mr Salway, Mr R. Mitchell, Mrs Hill, Mrs Edwards and Miss D. Brewer in the play "Awkward Mistake".

The Alphington Society of Ringers, with hand bells in 1924, had some well known faces amongst them including Rev Bennett, Messrs Rogers, Dymond, Coles, Brewer, Pike, Lake and Sanders.

A jolly ride for the children in 1940 was given on Mr Sidney Tout's horse and cart which was normally used to carry garden produce around the village. Mr Tout lived with his family on the site of Webb's garage (showroom) and then moved to a cottage on the corner of Mill Lane. On the cart left to right are (front row) Pearl Lake, unknown, Wendy Miller, (Back row) Roy Gibson, Tony Andrews, Barbara Melhuish, Pauline Bowdidge and Phillip Miller. This photo was taken outside Mile End Cottage.

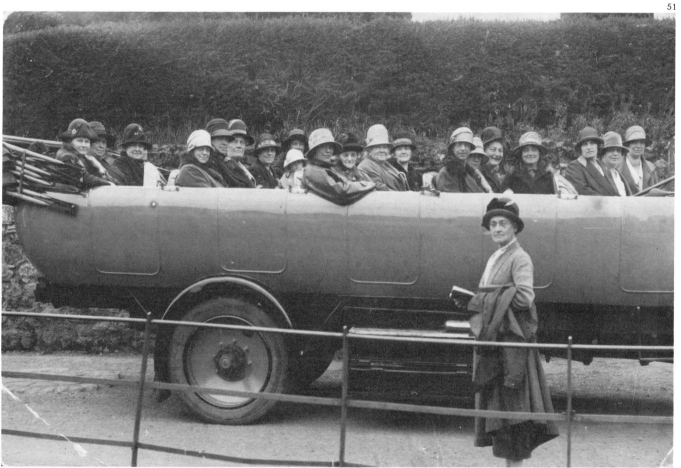

Here are the Alphington Mothers Union off for an outing. Standing is Mrs Webb (Harry Webb's mother) and also in the picture are Mesdames Evans (from Belvoir, Chudleigh Road), Coles, West, Marks, Eva and Alice Stone.

The headquarters of the Alphington ARP was at The Lodge, the home of Dr and Mrs Craig, and they were under the control of Newton Abbot. (Dr R. N. Craig was Master of the Stoke Hill Beagles and held the opening meet of the season here in 1936.) Their most serious call was to Dunsford where a German plane had been shot down and two badly burned German Airmen were moved by ambulance, actually an Alphington Laundry Van, to an

THE LODGE. 24067

Hotel in North Bovey which was being used as a Hospital during the war. Alphington played host to evacuees in the Second World War when 40 children were brought by train from Bristol and John Ruskin School, London to find a temporary home away from the bombing. The villagers welcomed them into their homes and they soon settled down to life in the village.

Before the war Alphington was lucky to have the help of Miss Marjorie Jago who conducted the Alphington Village Mixed Choir. The picture shows a combined mixed choir with some singers from Seaton and Sidmouth. The concert was held in a marquee in the Rectory grounds in 1938, the music was Vaughan Williams' 'Windsor Forest' and they were conducted by Vaughan Williams. The main vocalists were Isobel Baillie, Heddle Nash and Roy Henderson. Mrs Matthew was Leader of the Orchestra.

The picture shows the W. I. Choir and Junior Folk Dancers' play in 1947, taken in the garden of Pixie Cottage, the home of Mrs Goodman the Producer. The play was entitled "A Tale on the early Constable of Alphington". Mrs E. Coles, back row left, played the Constable, he being a member of the Coles family.

This picture shows the last practice of the Alphington Choral Society before going to London to sing under the Baton of Sir Adrian Boult in 1938. They rehearsed under Lionel Woodgates in the afternoon. Miss Jago is in the centre with the bouquet and, on her right, is Mrs Mitchell, aged 80, who was interviewed for the BBC.

The Horticultural Show was organised in 1938 to raise money for the Choir. The event was held in the garden of Belleville, the home of Dr R. Fortescue Foulkes and Dr Mary Foulkes. Miss Jago is fifth from the left in the second row wearing spectacles and Dr Mary Foulkes is second from the right in the third row.

This poor boy (a young Moxey now somewhat older!) seems to be quite happy to be used to 'beat the bounds' in 1958. The Rector, Rev Hammond-Croft is seen in the centre of the picture with Mr Moxey and his son prior to the start of Beating the Bounds. Also in the picture are: Messrs Moxey, Williams, Lake, Paton and son, Robinson, Brewer, Goodman, Selley, Mesdames Marks, Melhuish.

Twenty years earlier the walk of some 20 miles took 11 hours. The parish extended from Matford Brook in the east to the Lamb Inn, Longdown and Nadder Brook in the west, and included Wheatley, Rolls and Pocombe Bridges, Double Locks and Salmon Pool to which Clapperbrook Lane used to lead. The parish is shaped like an hour glass, the narrowest part being between the Villages of Alphington and Ide.

Alphington Football Team, 1956/7 Winners of the Devon County F. A. Junior Cup. Left to right (back row): Pike, Pill, Aplin, Bradford, Jarrett, Soper, Taylor, (front row): Clatworthy, Branson, Hall, Finch and Bunce.

Alphington AFC 1937/38 season. Left to right (back row): G. F. Marles, B. Davey (Vice-President), A. G. Wills, E. H. Robinson, P. E. Beale, Rev B. C. Bennett (President), Dr R. K. Foulkes (Vice-President), W. A. Wills (Chairman), A. G. Narramore, F. G. Coles (Vice-President), J. J. Brewer (Vice-President), (centre row): H. Cox, A. Moxey (Hon. Treas.), H. Brewer (Sub-Capt), W. Burge (Hon. Sec), G. Atkins, L. Wills (front row): S. Budd, W. Dymond, A. Courtney, W. Selley (Capt), H. Branton, F. Marles, W. Edwards.

Alphington Cricket Team 1955. Left to right (back row) Joy Baskerville (Scorer), P. Branson, F. Selley, Griffin, Gardner, S. Branson, W. Jones, L. Hawke (Umpire), (front row): Holland, Parr, S. Jones, Mr Storey, R. Selley and Gilpin.

Alphington and Exeter Ladies Netball Teams in the playing fields in 1956. Left to right: Mesdames Holman, Sharpe, Chamberlain, Pauline Coles, Diamond, Hogg, Penhaligan and Pam Coles. In the background is one of the two nissan huts erected in the playing fields during the war to house the RAF who manned a barrage balloon in the field. These huts were used after the war for Sports and Social events for which they were ideally suited being equipped with running water and washing facilities.

Ring out the old and ring in the new! In these pages we have had just a brief glimpse of people and places in our Alphington Album. The village is growing every year and the hills and meadows we knew so well as children, are now under houses and factories. Today's young generation of Alphingtonians will have their own memories and who knows what changes they will see in their lifetimes. We hope you have enjoyed our nostalgic look back through the years and if you are too young to remember it for yourself, hope you have been fascinated by how things were in the past in Alphington.